MR ENGLAND

Richard Bean

MR ENGLAND

OBERON BOOKS
LONDON

WWW.OBERONBOOKS.COM

First published in 2000 by Oberon Books Ltd

This electronic edition published in 2011 by Oberon Books Ltd
521 Caledonian Road, London N7 9RH
Tel: +44 (0) 20 7607 3637 / Fax: +44 (0) 20 7607 3629
e-mail: info@oberonbooks.com
www.oberonbooks.com

A catalogue record for this book is available from the British
Library.

ISBN: 978-1-84002-170-7

Visit www.oberonbooks.com to read more about all our books
and to buy them. You will also find features, author interviews and
news of any author events, and you can sign up for e-newsletters
so that you're always first to hear about our new releases.

www.bloomsbury.com

Set

An unenclosed space. The floor is made up of grey, concrete, motorway sections. Three lanes separated by white lines. Each lane has a run of black where oil from engines has over the years dripped and stained the road, and been run in. A tyre skid runs from lane two to lane one. A torn off piece of lorry tyre lies on the extreme stage right. Extreme stage left, a hub cap. The road continues into the back wall and into the distance. Down-stage right is an old, comfortable, black leather, swivel armchair. Down-stage left is a smaller, modern, light wood, Ikeaish, chair in primary colours. Up-stage right is a dining table chair with a table and sewing machine. The table is small, and dedicated to sewing. Up-stage left is an old, and worn, chintzy armchair. A small coffee table is set up-stage centre. It has opened and unopened post on it. Props are to be kept to a minimum, except where they are indispensable to the action.

Characters

STEPHEN ENGLAND
early forties

JUDITH ENGLAND
early forties

IRENE ENGLAND
seventy-five

ANDY
nineteen

Mr England was first performed at the Crucible Theatre, Sheffield in a co-production between the Crucible Theatre and the Royal National Theatre Studio, on 31 October 2000, with following cast:

STEPHEN, Neil McCaul

JUDITH, Jane Gurnett

IRENE, Avril Elgar

ANDY, Laurence Mitchell

Director Paul Miller

Designer Jackie Brooks

ACT ONE

The set is lit as the audience take their seats. To open, the lights go to black. During the blackout JUDITH, IRENE and ANDY take their seats. ANDY downstage left; JUDITH, upstage right; and IRENE, upstage left. The lights come up focused on STEPHEN ENGLAND as he walks from up-stage centre quickly and purposefully towards his chair down-stage right. STEPHEN ENGLAND is a man of 44, but looks older. He is solid, six feet tall, with greying hair and a neat businessman's haircut. He wears a two piece off the peg business suit with a rather faded Remembrance Day poppy in it, black shoes, a pink shirt with a white collar, a joke tie (The Simpsons, or Mickey Mouse), joke socks (Simpsons/Star Wars/ Disney). He has a signet ring on his left hand, and a sub-Rolex silver watch on his left wrist.

STEPHEN: (*On the phone.*) …three hundred one point six mil soffit cleats…two thousand MF thirteen panhead screws…two thousand twenty-five mil dry wall screws… five hundred G-six skirting plates …I know, I told them. They'll just have to send them back…two hundred three-point-six deep flange channels…one hundred three-point-six extra deep flange channels…and one, get this, one, Kelly's eye, the number one, one three-point-six ultra deep flange channel…they must have a problem there. They don't want any more board. They've got enough twelve mil gyp to partition China.
(*He flicks the mobile closed, and sits in the leather chair and talks to his therapist.*)
Stephen England. English Gypsum. Prefabricated building products division. Sector five customer liaison. Worked for Gypsum on and off for twenty-two years. Dad to twin daughters, Hannah and Jane. Forty-four years old. Wife number two, Judith, Jude. (*Beat.*)
Wednesday night, middle of the night. I got up, went downstairs, living room, had a shit on the mat, and pissed on the sofa. Wife gets up – cancels coffee morning, starts blubbing. Leaves home. Takes the car. Wife puts petrol in the car. It's a diesel. Car fucked, excuse my French. The

AA bring wife and car back. Wife gets a bus, goes to her mother's. Car buggered, can't go to work. Ring in and book a day's holiday. Never had a day off sick. I've never done anything like this before. (*Beat.*)

Dublin. I was in Dublin once, ha! I'm not going to Ireland again, one big open air asylum, you'd have your work cut out there pal. Gypsum launch of the High Impact Firewall system. It's ordinary gyp plasterboard, but it's laminated, and fire-proof – clever stuff. Can we shift it? No we can't. First night there I get legless with Des Stafford. He's alright is Des, you can have a laugh with him, he's done the job, you wimme? Result – I go to bed a bit under the influence. Hotel room. Middle of the night. Need a leak, there's no en-suite toilet – Ireland remember – I can't be bothered to walk down the hall, so I go in the sink on the side. Wake up in the morning – there is no sink in the side. All my papers are ruined. Learnt a big lesson there I did. Never buy white furniture. But Wednesday – I wasn't drunk. I knew what I was doing, sort of. Why did I do it?

(*Pause.*)

Dunno.

(*STEPHEN frowns fiercely.*

Lights up on the full set. STEPHEN remains glued in his frown, facing the audience. JUDITH sits at the sewing machine. She is not making anything. She is a 42-year-old good-looking woman with just a touch of grey in her hair. She wears pastel shades of wool, and catalogue clothes which veer dangerously towards the flowery, but just manage to remain subtle. Sitting in his chair downstage left is ANDY. He is 19. He wears tracksuit bottoms, a poofed up, anorak of fluorescent yellow nylon, and a floppy, white with blue hoops, Noddy-style hat.)

JUDITH: This book is dedicated to women and girls,
and especially to teachers of sewing everywhere,
who enjoy the feel of fabric,
the beauty of textiles,
the precision of stitches,
the smoothness of seams,

and who delight always in appropriate fabrics carefully cut
and made up for a happy purpose.

ANDY: Wassat?

JUDITH: It's the only poem I ever learnt. It's not a poem really.
In the book it says it's a dedication. My sewing teacher
gave me the Singer sewing manual when I left school.
I was the only girl to do the 'O' level. Miss Nicholas.
Unfortunate name for a teacher, especially a young
attractive one. She married one of the boys from the sixth
form. Quite a shock at the time. They live in Quorn now,
very nice. They've got five children, a double garage, and a
Mexican hairless.

ANDY: I wanna garage.

JUDITH: John Kray! I kissed him once. I went rather wild in
my twenties. Stephen doesn't know it all. Ha! I went to
Poland and lived in a squat with some very nice hippies,
Polish hippies. I'm ashamed of some of the things I did
then.

ANDY: Lot of boyfriends yeah?

JUDITH: I was one of the very few people who looked good
in an Afghan, and I'd worked out a way of getting rid of
the smell before you wore it. But you don't know what I'm
talking about do you – Afghans.

ANDY: Afghanistan innit?

JUDITH: No it's not. Don't worry about it. But Polish men.
Ugh. They all think they're gods. I came back to England
in the end. I prefer English men. They're not gods, but
they're not completely bananas either. Oh yes, I had
quite a go at everything in my twenties. You should make
the most of that time Andrew, don't try and grow up too
quickly, you might not like it when you do.

ANDY: What did Steve do in his twenties?

JUDITH: He sold an awful lot of half-inch plaster board.

ANDY: I wanna lot of girlfriends. A garage and a lot of
girlfriends. Maybe a double garage.

JUDITH: I met him at a rugby club disco. He had mistletoe
sticking out of his flies. He thought it was funny. So did
I. It wasn't even Christmas. When I knew it was twins I

resigned from United Sugars. It was a good job as well. Better money than Stephen's. You haven't got a car have you Andy?

ANDY: Soon innit?

JUDITH: Ooh, how exciting.

ANDY: Got a job now. Compu'ers.

JUDITH: Oh, that's wonderful news Andy. A job!

ANDY: That's why I come round innit.

JUDITH: Oh, smashing! Stephen will be pleased for you.

ANDY: Yeah.

JUDITH: A job. Gosh. Lovely.

ANDY: I wanna borrow his jigsaw. (*Beat.*) Smells of piss in 'ere. Wassat? The old gal?

JUDITH: Good heavens no. The cat. Last week.

ANDY: I don't remember no cat. Where's the twins?

JUDITH: They're in Austria, skiing with the Catholics. They've only been gone two days and I miss them already. Stephen says I've got to toughen up.

ANDY: How long?

JUDITH: Two weeks.

ANDY: I'm supposed to be a Caflic.

JUDITH: Oh we're only educational Catholics, so they can go to that school. When they go to secondary school we'll have a relapse I imagine. They're all Catholic in Poland. Real Catholics. Except the Jews.

ANDY: What are they?

JUDITH: The Jews?

ANDY: Yeah.

JUDITH: Jewish.

ANDY: 'course.

(*ANDY lights a cigarette.*)

Do you smoke Mrs England?

JUDITH: No.

ANDY: Have you ever smoked?

JUDITH: No.

ANDY: Have you ever fought about taking it up?

JUDITH: No.

ANDY: Just that now would be a good time. (*Beat.*)

(*He takes out from under his jacket a huge 200 box of Marlboro Lights.*)

Mate of mine's a smuggler. Two hundred Marlboro Lites. Ten quid. Belgian.

JUDITH: We used to smoke marijuana in the squats in Poland. You can call me Judith. I've known you for five years, and you're nearly a man now. You've got a job, that's a start.

ANDY: Just a little suck?

JUDITH: Just one.

(*JUDITH goes to ANDY and stands by his chair. ANDY takes a cigarette from the huge box and lights it, takes a drag to get it going, and then gives it to JUDITH. JUDITH takes a drag, and enjoys it.*)

JUDITH: Ooh. It makes you tingle doesn't it?

ANDY: Is he at work?

JUDITH: No, he's in the garage. Watching one of his war videos. I won't have it in the house.

ANDY: He's got a vid in the garage?

JUDITH: Don't tell anyone or we'll be burgled.

(*Enter IRENE ENGLAND. She is a 75-year-old woman. She wears a quality tweed skirt and a silk top. There is a whiff of Bohemia, but only a whiff. She carries an old and very large hard-back copy of Brewer's Phrase and Fable. She stands centre stage.*)

IRENE: Oh it's you again is it Andrew?

ANDY: No.

IRENE: (*To ANDY.*) Stephen's bought a new answerphone and put a stupid message on it. Ring us up when we're out and listen to it.

(*To JUDITH.*) Still smells of his doings in here. Has he cleaned it up? Has he heckers like. You had a go didn't you?

(*To ANDY.*) You'd think that Germaine Greer had never written a book with her.

JUDITH: (*To IRENE.*) It was the cat.

IRENE: There must be something very seriously wrong with the cat that made the mess I saw.

(*To ANDY.*) Stephen got up in the middle of the night and peed all over the carpet and then did a number two on the mat. Something must have upset him. I went to that car boot sale at the rugby ground on Sunday lots of people ooh you couldn't move for rubbish some chap had a poetry anthology but he said it had been on the floor of his basement and it had flooded so I asked him if he had any dry poetry. That threw him. Some poems maybe that he'd been keeping above the level of the water table in his loft maybe but he said he kept his books in the basement and his tools in the loft well that's a man who's living his life upside down if you ask me I said to him you want your head examining he said to me, 'Fuck off you old fish!', well ask yourself how much poetry are you going to sell if you talk to people like that.

ANDY: I was there innit. I wanted a ratchet screwdriver. Always a lot of tools at them fings. Some good stuff, nicked some of it innit. Couldn't see anyfin'.

(*Pause.*)

IRENE: You should read more poetry, it helped me, it still helps me, actually it's essential. My Brewer's Dictionary I've had it

ANDY: – firty-five years. And you've got all the good words underlined.

JUDITH: Stephen might have a ratchet screwdriver Andrew.

(*IRENE sits in the chair up-stage left.*)

ANDY: Sorted innit.

JUDITH: Oh good. Making progress with it then? The thing.

ANDY: Coming on. I need a jigsaw – I know he's got one.

IRENE: Stephen likes his garage it's tidy like a room and everything's got labels on it I've seen 'plane' but I haven't seen 'jigsaw' the car's not in there at the moment because Judith put petrol in it and it's a diesel one works by a spark and one is continuous combustion two different systems and you can't mix them up it's at the garage. I drove a lorry during the war, it's easy enough, but you've got to remember that it's big. Elvis Presley drove a lorry, but he was never any good after his mother died. Mario Lanza was good too, but he used to relieve himself into a bucket on the set, upset a lot of people that did. Especially his wife. Maybe that's where Stephen got the idea. Mario Lanza lost it too like Elvis, after his mother died. They all do. All the greats. Elvis, Mario Lanza, Roy Orbison, Cliff Richards. As soon as the mother goes, they lose all feeling, and if you haven't feeling you can't sing.

JUDITH: Cliff Richard's mother is still alive. I saw her on telly the other night.

IRENE: Is she? Ha! You wait.

JUDITH: I don't know why you don't like Cliff? He's nice.

IRENE: I don't like him for the same reason I don't keep a bucket of sick in the corner of my room.

ANDY: Steve's car's diesel innit?

JUDITH: The Vectra, yes. I put petrol in it.

IRENE: They had a big row about it all marriages are up and down you've got to work at them I married mine out of pity, he's dead now. I'm not putting flowers on his grave he never gave me flowers.

JUDITH: I'm going to make a pot of tea. Andrew? Tea?

ANDY: Yeah. Ta.

JUDITH: Irene?

IRENE: I had one at about three, and I haven't been since, so I'll need to go soon, so a cup of tea might help. Yes.

(*JUDITH exits stage left. ANDY immediately stands and goes round behind IRENE and picks up the copy of Brewer's and slips it into his coat. He then sits back down.*)

I don't go to doctors anymore the one I saw last he hardly looked at me he was looking at his computer screen he asked me if I had a problem with my plumbing he used that word 'plumbing' I mean a doctor an educated man hasn't got the guts to call a spade a spade he'd be better off as a plumber it's forty pounds call out now just to have a look at a washing machine they earn more than footballers some plumbers more than those footballers in the lower divisions. That Muslim lad was good who played for Leicester City but he's left now his father's a firemen I bet his mother wasn't let out the house they have to wear

the veil you know. It's so the men don't get frisky – huh!
There's madness behind closed doors.

(*Enter STEPHEN. He goes straight to pick up his post from the
coffee table. He stands centre stage leafing through it.*)

STEPHEN: (*Friendly, blokey.*) Eh up there's a burglar.

ANDY: Alright.

STEPHEN: More than alright pal. They've given me a rental
car. A bloody Alfa Romeo. Wa hey! I tell you, that rev
counter hasn't dropped below fifty thousand RPM all day.

ANDY: Italian innit?

STEPHEN: Goes like taramasalata off a shovel.

ANDY: Taramasalata's Greek.

STEPHEN: Same difference.

IRENE: She's been cleaning your pee up. Are you alright now
love?

STEPHEN: Musn't grumble.

IRENE: Apple crumble. We used to say that all the time musn't
grumble apple crumble I like apple crumble it's easier to
make than you think it's best if you use apples. He wants to
borrow your jigsaw.

STEPHEN: Never thought of getting a job, saving up and
buying one.

ANDY: I've got a job.

STEPHEN: Bloody hell! What? You've done a day's work and it
hasn't killed you?

ANDY: Computers innit?

STEPHEN: (*To ANDY.*) What sort of company doesn't mind you
going to work looking like a bloody lampshade?

ANDY: Friday's you wear what you like.

STEPHEN: Ha! Eh Mum, you can wear what you like on a
Friday now.

IRENE: I go to Leicester on a Friday. You can wear what you
like in Leicester.

ANDY: Can I borrow it? The jigsaw.

STEPHEN: 'Borrow' is a commie word. 'Buy.' That's the word
you're looking for. One month of solid borrowing and the
British economy would collapse. Two months and we'll
all be eating pickled beetroot, shagging our sisters and

drinking petrol. My father didn't lay down his life for this country so that you could go around borrowing things instead of buying them. Eighteen he was when he went off to fight Rommel. Chalk and gorgonzola, you and my old dad. Drugs, tracksuits, women. He'd never heard of 'em.

IRENE: He didn't die.

ANDY: He weren't killed. I know he weren't.

STEPHEN: That's what I said. I said he didn't lay down his life –

ANDY: You've lost it mate.

STEPHEN: I haven't finished! If it wasn't for men like him do you know what you'd be doing now?

ANDY: What? What would I be doing now?

STEPHEN: Something very German.

IRENE: Leave him alone. He came round to borrow some power tools and you're going on about your dad like as if he was a war hero or something when you know very well he surrendered in north Africa and spent all his time in a holiday camp in Italy.

STEPHEN: He escaped from that 'holiday camp' three times!

IRENE: They didn't have a fence. He spent three years in a village with an Itii girl and just went down to the camp on a Monday morning to sign on. He came back with some very funny ideas.

STEPHEN: You're just dead against him because you married him.

(*To ANDY.*) Go on then it's in the garage. Blades are in a box marked 'blades jig'.

ANDY: Yeah, I know.

STEPHEN: What are you mekkin?

ANDY: An 'ole innit?

STEPHEN: Stupid question.

(*ANDY exits stage left. He closes the door behind him.*)

When did Jude come back?

IRENE: This morning. She's ruined the carpet. She used bleach.

(*Enter JUDITH.*)

JUDITH: (*To STEPHEN.*) Is the siege of Stalingrad over?

STEPHEN: Yeah, 'bout five minutes ago.

JUDITH: (*Sharply.*) Well make yourself useful set the dinner table. Four places. Soup, and a main course. You can pour the tea too. Andrew has two sugars, your mother has white without and I don't want any – I'm too busy making dinner.

(*JUDITH glares at him, and exits via stage left. ANDY enters from stage left carrying a jigsaw in a cardboard box.*)

STEPHEN: (*To IRENE.*) Good. We're talking again.

IRENE: You found the jigsaw then, in the garage?

ANDY: No.

STEPHEN: D'yer know Andy. That woman is the Rolls Royce of women. I should know I've had a few second hand Cortinas. And it isn't what you see is what you get. Ask her about Poland. She's done some things in Poland that most women can only dream about. Incredible things, just one woman she was, a young woman, and three hundred hairy arsed Polish blokes. You ask her about it, it's incredible. You've gotta be careful with women though Andy. Now you've got a job they'll all be sniffing round. What I was doing with my first marriage I do not know. Take my advice, if you ever think of marrying put your dick in the fridge for a week and do your bloody homework. Check her family out. If you find either cancer, madness, or communism – chuck your cards in. I got a praal of shit with the first one. Eh, gimme that.

(*He takes the jigsaw from its box and looks at it carefully. He puts it back and returns it to ANDY. Enter JUDITH.*)

Just wanted a look, 'cos I'll never see it again.

ANDY: Tomorrow innit?

JUDITH: It's a vegetable soup Andy, so you can eat it. We're going to have lamb chops but I'll put some oven chips in for you.

ANDY: Ta.

(*Exit JUDITH stage left.*)

I'm seeing a woman.

STEPHEN: You see, life begins when you start paying taxes. Job, girl, what else is there? – flat, you'll be getting a flat next. Wa! Hey! Who is she?

(*JUDITH enters. She has taken her pinafore off and has put on some lipstick, and ear rings. This is noticed by STEPHEN, who thinks it's unusual but he doesn't say anything.*)

JUDITH: It's all in the oven.

IRENE: Have you never eaten meat Andrew?

ANDY: It's uneffical innit?

STEPHEN: You wouldn't recognise an ethic if it jumped into bed with you and nicked the duvet.

IRENE: We used to call them eiderdowns after the duck.

STEPHEN: Do you know why I eat meat? Reward. Monday to Friday I'm on that road working my testicles into a frenzy –

JUDITH: Stephen! Language!

STEPHEN: – working my balls into a frenzy selling prefabricated building products to people who don't want them. One of the few luxuries I allow myself is organically farmed meat. My meat, Andrew, has been frollicking around the Vale of Belvoir, roaming the most beautiful bastard acres of this beautiful bastard island of ours, totally and completely shag happy. Suddenly, one day, when they're asleep, exhausted from all the laughing and clapping, they are turned into lamb chops. Do you know why they've been given the chance to exist?

ANDY: Yeah.

STEPHEN: 'cos I'm gonna eat them.

JUDITH: Leave him alone Stephen.

STEPHEN: There is, however, one little lamb called Fluffy, who hasn't been invited to the party. She has been knocking on the door of this endless rave for years, but Fluffy will never be allowed in. Why? Because you, you selfish bastard, are a bloody vegetarian! I don't know how you kids sleep at nights.

IRENE: I count sheep.

(*JUDITH and ANDY laugh.*)

STEPHEN: Very funny. Eh Jude, miladdo's met a woman.

JUDITH: Oh lovely.

ANDY: Yeah.

JUDITH: Oh smashing. Well, well. That's lovely.

ANDY: She's older than me innit?

STEPHEN: Wa hey! The older woman.

IRENE: Is she nice?

ANDY: Yeah.

STEPHEN: You don't want a nice girl, not at your age. You want someone who's been round the block already.

JUDITH: That's enough Stephen.

STEPHEN: Someone who will deliver the goods without you having to get down on your knees in a bus shelter sobbing with lust, begging for a bit just to keep you going.

(*JUDITH stands and exits to the kitchen. STEPHEN notices. During the next STEPHEN takes his socks off and starts inspecting his feet.*)

Something I said. D'yer know much about the siege of Stalingrad? Course you don't. You're pig ignorant. Germans surrounded. Winter. They all wore leather and it was wet so they stank of wet leather. I'll lend you the videos.

IRENE: He's got his feet out! Put your feet away. I'm not staying in here with them feet.

(*STEPHEN gives her a 'Your choice then' look. IRENE sighs and leaves. As she leaves she looks for her copy of Brewer's on the coffee table.*)

STEPHEN: You ever thought of the army? Territorials.

ANDY: Busy, weekends.

STEPHEN: I bet.

IRENE: Where's my Brewer's?

STEPHEN: You'll have left it upstairs.

IRENE: I brought it down, and put it on there.

STEPHEN: Upstairs!

(*IRENE exits. During the next the lighting gradually lowers and focusses on ANDY and STEPHEN down-stage. ANDY leads STEPHEN down-stage and with confidence lights a cigarette.*)

They wouldn't have me, the Terries.

ANDY: Dodgy back.

STEPHEN: Disc problems.

ANDY: Eye trouble.

STEPHEN: Have I told you? They wouldn't let me drive a tank at night. They said I might be dangerous. I thought that was the whole point of a tank.

ANDY: Athlete's foot.

STEPHEN: They weren't bothered about that. Could be useful in war – athlete's foot. Peace and war. Two different sets of demands. Peace.

ANDY: Tell me.

STEPHEN: Working for Gypsum.

ANDY: On the road meeting clients.

STEPHEN: Little chef.

ANDY: Pancakes, maple syrup.

STEPHEN: Diary, mobile, knowledge of the building game.

ANDY: Vauxhall Vectra, Derek and the Dominoes, smell of your own farts.

STEPHEN: The clients.

ANDY: Bastards.

STEPHEN: Architechts.

ANDY: Middle class bastards.

STEPHEN: Graduates.

ANDY: The customer is always wrong.

STEPHEN: You remembered that, good.

ANDY: They're fucking stupid!

STEPHEN: They say they want bog standard twelve mil gyp but –

ANDY: They don't know what they want.

STEPHEN: They 'need' fifteen mil high impact thermal laminate.

ANDY: Need and want.

STEPHEN: Two different human motivators.

ANDY: Athlete's foot.

STEPHEN: I'm coming to that. It's a new product.

ANDY: A risk.

STEPHEN: They're sticking their necks out.

ANDY: It's more expensive.

STEPHEN: It's thicker.

ANDY: They're scared.

STEPHEN: They order twelve mil gyp.

ANDY: Again.

STEPHEN: They're stupid.

ANDY: They're not sticking their necks out.

STEPHEN: Bastards.

ANDY: Cunts.

STEPHEN: You laugh, have a drink, take the piss. But you don't get close.

ANDY: Intimacy.

STEPHEN: They don't get to know about your family, your wife, your problems. But in a war situation.

(*During the next the lighting lowers further.*)

ANDY: Bunker.

STEPHEN: It's cold.

ANDY: Basement.

STEPHEN: You haven't eaten for days.

ANDY: Bridge.

STEPHEN: You godda hold the bridge.

ANDY: Ammo running low.

STEPHEN: No food.

ANDY: No water.

STEPHEN: Reinforcements are not expected.

ANDY: The kid's crying.

STEPHEN: Morale is slipping.

ANDY: Who's the leader?

STEPHEN: I'm the leader.

ANDY: Course you are Stevie.

STEPHEN: Whaddyer do?

ANDY: Take your boots off.

STEPHEN: There's a smell.

ANDY: A fucking stink.

STEPHEN: Athlete's foot.

ANDY: There it is.

STEPHEN: You crack a joke about cheese.

ANDY: It's funny.

STEPHEN: The platoon are knit more closely.

ANDY: A waterproof cardigan.

STEPHEN: Intimacy.

ANDY: The kid stops crying.

STEPHEN: Bingo!

ANDY: You've won the fucking war.

(*ANDY offers a cigarette to STEPHEN. They smoke together like buddies in a platoon.*
Silence.)

ANDY: You got it on both feet?

STEPHEN: Yeah. But they don't call it athlete's feet. Technically what I've got is athlete's foot – twice. War tests a man. Peace? You're lucky if you get one chance in a whole bloody lifetime. I have this dream, a recurring dream. I'm a wolf.

ANDY: Big, hairy bollocked wolf.

STEPHEN: Battle scarred.

ANDY: One ear.

STEPHEN: Fur missing.

ANDY: One eye.

STEPHEN: Teeth.

ANDY: One leg.

STEPHEN: Come on! I'm the leader.

ANDY: The boss, number one, top dog.

STEPHEN: Canada.

ANDY: Snow, lakes, dead boring.

STEPHEN: We're starving.

ANDY: The bitches are hungry.

STEPHEN: It's up to me.

ANDY: Do something!

STEPHEN: The buffalo –

ANDY: Buffalo?!

STEPHEN: Yeah, buffalo. The buffalo are not where they should be.

ANDY: Clever buffalo.

STEPHEN: I say we go north.

ANDY: But it's cold.

STEPHEN: A young wolf.

ANDY: Young, fit, hairy bollocks.

STEPHEN: Challenges my leadership.

ANDY: You fight him off.

STEPHEN: We go north.

ANDY: Looking for buffalo.

STEPHEN: It's getting colder.

ANDY: It would do – you're going north.

STEPHEN: We find them.

ANDY: All day breakfast.

STEPHEN: I see an old bull.

ANDY: Gammy leg.

STEPHEN: Slow.

ANDY: Foam rubber horns.

STEPHEN: We sideline him.

ANDY: On the wing.

STEPHEN: Separate him.

ANDY: Surround him.

STEPHEN: Kill him.

ANDY: Eat him.

STEPHEN: I am appreciated.

ANDY: By the women.

STEPHEN: The women, the young, the old.

ANDY: But mainly the women.

(*Lights up.*)

STEPHEN: Strategy, tactics, moment. That's what men are good at. Not this other shit.

ANDY: You saved my life innit?

STEPHEN: I was lucky Andy. Life gave me the chance, that moment, and I did the right thing.

(*Lights focus on STEPHEN in the therapist's chair.*)

Management assessment weekend, Gypsum. We're on an island in the middle of this lake. You had to get everybody off without anybody getting wet. No boats, no hovercraft, no string. I quickly established myself as the leader. Couple of graduates there an'all, huh, straight off the tit and into management. So, island, five of us, I'm in charge.

(*Silence.*)

They had to send a boat out in the end. Next up eighteen tins of nuclear waste – old paint tins actually – and you had to get all eighteen tins into this shed without anyone getting contaminated, touching the tins. I got myself established as leader again, no problem there, and I told one of the group, the one I'd earmarked as a liability, to go and pick all the tins up and put them in the shed. I'd made the tough decision to sacrifice one for the many. Very common in war that.

(*Pause.*)

Apparently, there was a way of doing it without anyone
getting contaminated – strings and sticks or something,
so we scored nothing there. The last exercise, I was just
assessing the problem, summarising, setting objectives
when one of the graduates took hold of me by the jumper.
He was brick shithouse big and he sat me down on this tree
trunk and he said, 'Sit here, shutup, or I'll shove this tree
trunk up your arse, sideways.' They did quite well in that
exercise.

(*Pause.*)

Look, last week was a one-off. I'd had a curry, a Ceylon,
they're hotter than you think you know.

(*Pause.*)

I've had a go at management. After the assessments I
joined Midland Aggregates as an Area Sales Manager.
Three litre Volvo. Cruise control, air con, ABS, side impact
bars. Kaw! clever little thing to put your coffee on.

(*Silence.*)

The whole company went down the bloody pan. I didn't
know where to bloody start. I just sat in my office and
ate crisps. You see, I know how to panic on the road.
You put your foot down, use the bus lanes, nip in behind
an ambulance. I went back to Gypsum. They gave me a
Cavalier. A one point four Vauxhall Cavalier, where you
jam your coffee between the handbrake and the passenger
seat. A fucking, bastard, shit, piece of shit fucking bastard
tin shite fucking Cavalier! (*Beat.*)

A yellow one!!

(*JUDITH approaches STEPHEN's chair. She puts her hands on
the chair, and then on to his shoulders.*)

JUDITH: You were a bit late tonight Steve.

STEPHEN: I had a bevvy at the club. The third fifteen work out
on a Wednesday night. Good bunch of lads, some nutters,
ha!

JUDITH: Are you alright?

STEPHEN: I dunno. I've never thought about it.

JUDITH: You're not alright are you?

(*He sits.*)

What did the psychologist say?

STEPHEN: Mmm. Mmmm. Mmmmmm. Mmmmmmmmmm. That's all he ever says. Bloody nodding dog. Maybe he can't talk. Just my luck eh? I get the dumb one. Maybe he's deaf as well.

JUDITH: Is he nice?

STEPHEN: They don't come any nicer. He's a poof.

JUDITH: He's gay?

STEPHEN: Yeah, he's a right girl-boy. Gave me a hug today. Kaw! I nearly shit myself. It's the buggery I can't stand. The thought of it. Ugh!

JUDITH: You've got a short memory Steve.

STEPHEN: Eh?

JUDITH: That time in Belgium. We were staying in that little hotel run by nuns. Seven years ago. You asked if you could do it then, to me. You wanted to put it up my backside.

STEPHEN: What are you talking about?

JUDITH: Belgium. Buggery.

STEPHEN: What?

JUDITH: Don't tell me you don't remember!?

STEPHEN: That was different.

JUDITH: Why?

STEPHEN: We were on holiday! (*Beat.*) It wasn't just Belgium, it was Ypres.

JUDITH: Did you talk about us?

STEPHEN: Gypsum. Do you next week mebbe.

JUDITH: I've been thinking about what you did, and maybe it's because of us. Maybe we should have a holiday.
(*STEPHEN stands and walks away from her.*)

STEPHEN: We've just had a holiday. Neuve Chappelle. Brilliant, eh Jude? The Frogs, I know I don't like 'em, but at the end of the day when all's said and done, you've godda give it to 'em – they've done our boys proud. That grass was like a bloody snooker table!

JUDITH: I mean a proper holiday Steve. Not visiting war cemeteries. A beach. I want to make love to you Steve in a hotel, in a big bed, on stiff linen sheets, and I want us both to be a bit tipsy on our dessert wine, Montbassillac, and to laugh a lot.

STEPHEN: The tent's brand new.

JUDITH: I don't want a sleeping bag on the ground next to you in a separate single sleeping bag –

STEPHEN: I'll get one of those big double air beds. Bed on a shelf they're called. Innovations report. I've got a tyre pump.

JUDITH: (*Rising.*) – in a tent in a field surrounded by thousands and thousands of dead young boys!

(*Silence.*)

I want a beach.

STEPHEN: Gallipoli. Turkey, the Dardanelles.

(*STEPHEN turns and starts walking quickly to centre stage and then in a straight line towards a central point in the back wall. He raises his voice during the next, and shouts over his shoulder to JUDITH.*)

It's beautiful apparently. A lot of Lancashire lads died at Gallipoli, yeah you don't hear much about that do you? Yeah, we don't make a fuss about it like the Ossies. Yup, I'd like to go and pay my respects to those bloody heroes, those men.

JUDITH: Oh fuck them!

(*JUDITH turns and watches him go, and then takes her seat at the sewing machine. STEPHEN turns and walks back quickly, talking on his mobile phone. The lighting changes.*)

STEPHEN: (*On the phone.*) I dunno Des mate. He sacked the lift engineer on Tuesday…dunno, must've put it in sideways – No, they're buying twelve mil standard gyp… Look Des, I've done the demo, I attacked it with a lump hammer, set fire to the fucking thing and put the fire out with a cup of cocoa, but they're not impressed enough to buy… Yes it is public use, it's a council swimming bath…Des, Des, listen mate, they know the gyp board won't last ten minutes into the first school trip, but they're not buying the F Wall system, they're not interested. …Yeah…yeah…yeah, alright. I will, alright, I'll ring him. See you pal.

(*He flips the mobile closed.*)

Fuck!!!!

(*He sits in the leather chair and addresses his therapist.*)

My first wife had left me. Don't know why. She'd run off
with her diving instructor, bloke at the sub-aqua club.
Flash bastard, you know the type – Rolex, Armani suit,
flippers. So me and Roger – he's mad, Roger, you'd have
your work cut out there pal – boiler engineer. Switzerland.
Singles holiday. Big mistake. Dead as a dodo Switzerland.
The nearest talent is Czechoslovakia. Lake Lucerne. Cruise
ship. I've gone below to the restaurant to get the beers in.
Bang! Engine room goes up like a bloody bomb. The boat
lists to one side and the lake's coming in. This one porthole
is the only way out. So I stand on the end of the bar and
reach up to the porthole so the kids can climb up me like a
ladder and out. And Andy, that's the kid who comes round
our house, he's first out but there's no sign of his sister, his
mother or his dad. Five kids I saved. There's no one else
left alive in the bar and I pull myself out and into the water
and kick for the surface. When I get up to the top I can
see that Andy's struggling, thrashing around, so I grab this
football and give it to him like a float. Speedboat comes
along. Next thing I know I'm on the quay side, and this kid
said something in French and pointed me out. Le monsieur
qui a fait le pont, the bridge man. Thirty-two dead. Andy
lost his dad, his mom, and his sister. He's alright. Comes
round a lot. Typical teenager really. Bag of bones, no
muscles, won't go out if it's windy. He lost the lot. We
don't talk about it. Maybe he saw them die. Dunno. Best
forgotten eh? I was in the papers and I picked up a gong at
Buck Palace. Yeah, she's alright, the old Queenie, a good
laugh, really natural.

(*STEPHEN swivels his chair to direct his questions to IRENE.*)

(*To IRENE.*) Food, as a baby, was I 'A' breast fed; 'B' bottle
fed; or what else is there? I dunno.

IRENE: I started off trying to feed you myself but of course
you were difficult, you've always been difficult, nothing's
straightforward with you, if there's two options you'll go
and do the third, well you would feed from my left one

but you'd never feed from my right one and the doctors
said that was because my left one was bigger because of
all the typing because in those days we didn't have word
processors or computers so when you got to the end of
a line you had to go like that and that's why I've lost this
breast they never said that when they did the mastectomy
but that's what I think I've got used to it and people say
you can't tell. I can tell but I know of course so it's possible
that that's clouding my judgement. Have you seen my
Brewer's?

STEPHEN: So breast or bottle?

IRENE: Both and –

STEPHEN: Next. The birth. 'A' – natural, 'B' – forceps 'C'
– caesarian.

IRENE: You got halfway out on your own, but you were the
wrong way round, so they shoved you back in and turned
you round inside it was like a double decker bus doing
a three point turn in a washing machine you're always
talking about heroes and men and sacrifice well we didn't
have gas and air in those days no we just used to yell that's
why I didn't want any more –

STEPHEN: Is there any history of flipping in the family?
Nervous complaints. First, granddad, my dad's dad. 'A'
– yes, 'B' – no.

IRENE: When he died that was a spectacular flip. Hit by a
mobile library doing fifty miles an hour. Never read a book
in his life.

(*Enter ANDY.*)

STEPHEN: Thanks Mum.

IRENE: Hello Andrew, have you come to see us again?

ANDY: No.

(*Enter JUDITH.*)

STEPHEN: You can't stay I'm off to rugby in a mo.

JUDITH: Hello Andrew.

ANDY: Hello Judith.

STEPHEN: Judith? Who said you could call Mrs England
Judith?

JUDITH: He's working now. He's a man.

STEPHEN: Chasing a mouse about a bloody screen doesn't make you a man. Jigsaw alright?

(*ANDY reaches into his bag and takes out the boxed jigsaw and hands it to STEPHEN.*)

ANDY: Fings out innit.

STEPHEN: Fings out innit? Fings out innit? D'you hear that mother. Fings out innit. Language – the one thing that puts a bidda clear water between us and the bloody monkeys, and he hasn't got the hang of it yet.

IRENE: Poetry that's what you need. Have you seen my Brewer's?

STEPHEN: (*To JUDITH.*) Fings out innit. On the jigsaw.

JUDITH: (*To STEPHEN.*) The height gauge. Yes, you said that, last time you used it.

ANDY: Where you off?

STEPHEN: Rugby. Eh, and another thing. This is the twennie-first century you know, you ring up first, you don't just knock on the door and come in.

IRENE: I can still remember when you used to be able to leave your back door open, there was no thieving everybody knew everybody's business you'd just leave the door on the latch and you'd go in and you'd just say yoo hoo! That's instead of a doorbell yoo hoo! and nothing ever got stolen –

STEPHEN: That's cos you had bugger all worth nicking. I mean, who's gonna want to nick a tin bath, a slice of fried bread, and a bit of half finished tapestry? Eh? Think about it.

(*ANDY hands over two war videos.*)

ANDY: Brought your vids back.

STEPHEN: Good?

ANDY: First one's a bit boring.

STEPHEN: The First World War a bit boring?

JUDITH: Stop bullying him Steve.

ANDY: Black and white innit.

STEPHEN: They didn't have colour in those days. Did they mother?

IRENE: Don't talk to me like that. I was born in 1925.

STEPHEN: I know that. That's why I said 'they'.

IRENE: Of course they had colour. Everyone's always had colour.

STEPHEN: Eh? I mean film, television. Oh bloody hell. So, you weren't gripped by trench life then?

ANDY: That Passchendaele. Stupid innit?

STEPHEN: Oh yes, Passchendaele, that was stupid. A hundred and seventy thousand killed fighting for a village that was just brick dust.
(*To JUDITH.*) We've been there haven't we Jude! Passchendaele.

JUDITH: Yes. Three times. It's nice but there's nothing for the kids.

STEPHEN: (*To ANDY.*) Do you know why we held on at the third battle of Ypres? Because our lads, the ordinary working class lads of this country, were physically and mentally tough. God help this country if there's a call up today. Your lot'll surrender as soon as you find out khaki is itchy. At Passchendaele Tommy Atkins fired so fast the Germans thought they were facing machine guns. Oh yes, just a good bunch of lads, working for each other, highly trained, understanding the team work thing, brave, bloody gutsy.

ANDY: Strategy, tactics, moment.

STEPHEN: You remember – good. Bit like rugby. Fifteen men working together towards a common purpose.

JUDITH: Get out the way of the women for a couple of hours, and then get drunk.

STEPHEN: The line-outs right – if he's gonna throw the ball to me the hooker shouts 'Gizmo' – that's my call sign if you like. Communication.

ANDY: Gizmo?

STEPHEN: Comes from 'Gypsum', but half of the blokes in this league know I work for Gypsum so it can't be Gypsum.
(*To JUDITH.*) Eh Jude can you lend me twennie quid? I'm strapped for liquid.

JUDITH: No.

STEPHEN: Alright, alright. I'll get thirty from the corner.
(*STEPHEN turns to go.*)

ANDY: Can I borrow yer rasp?

STEPHEN: I knew it. I bloody knew it. You know where it is.
(*STEPHEN leaves, walking purposefully in a line from centre stage to a central point in the back wall.*)

ANDY: Don't he get on your tits?

IRENE: No. Anyway, I've only got one. Did you ring the answerphone when we were out? It's supposed to be a funny message that sort of thing's all very well like those Mickey Mouse telephones it's all very very funny when it rings and Mickey Mouse jumps about but when you answer it and they tell you that your father's died the joke sort of pales a little don't you think there's always bad news coming oh yes the bookies won't accept bets on that one they weren't married you know Mickey Mouse and Minnie Mouse no Walt Disney was always uncomfortable about that because he was a Christian and although they were only mice and obviously not real either he began to develop a guilt thing which killed him in the end.

ANDY: Did your dad fight in the war?

IRENE: He was on convoys. North Atlantic. He had an easy first war, in the second he wasn't so lucky he was making telephones on essential services but 'cos he looked young everyone gave him a hard time saying that he should be fighting the way people treated him you'd think he was German you don't wanna believe all that community codswallop about the war and all pulling together it was I'm alright Jack and go to hell you bastard he became very depressed and he volunteered in the end and joined ENSA, 'cos he had a good singing voice and did a bit of magic, he picked up an infection from one of his doves and died in Tunis. Edgar Alan Padgett like Edgar Allan Poe but Padgett instead of Poe

ANDY: Edgar Alan Padgett. Padgett.

IRENE: You're always round here aren't you?

ANDY: Yeah.

IRENE: You should read more poetry.

ANDY: Eh?

JUDITH: Leave him alone Irene.

IRENE: You'd pick up a few words. Brewer's Dictionary of
Phrase and Fable. I'm virtually dependent on it I have to
read it every day some folks need insulin it's part of my
treatment when I say I read it every day I can't find it at
the moment. I'm feeling funny words are flying about
inside my head and then there's nothing like a big window
I didn't used to read all of it each day day, that would be
nearly impossible certainly impossible on a Friday because
I go to Leicester –

JUDITH: Andrew doesn't want to know about that Irene.

ANDY: She's told me innit. Brewer's. Under Milk Wood.

IRENE: See. Oh yes, I have to have a love of words although
with me it's not natural I'm not a born lover of poetry,
Under Milk Wood's one of my poems. But poems feed that
skill, the facility of speaking. If I don't have my Brewer's
and my poetry the will will – that's two wills – will atrophy,
sounds like a sneeze, atrophy but it is actually another
good word, it means to wither on the vine, which is a
metaphor about grapes or raisins, depending on whether
it's before or after.

(*ANDY stands and goes and takes a wad of post from off the
sideboard. This he stuffs into his jacket. He then goes back and
sits down on the sofa.*)

ANDY: (*Whispered.*) Under Milk Wood ain't a poem. It's a play
innit.

IRENE: I know that that's what he called it, but it's poetry
really I don't like rhyming I think it's silly but I do like
metaphors, alliteration, similes though I find similes
disappointing, like melted ice-cream, that's a simile and
you wouldn't believe this Andrew there was a time when I
didn't say a word to anybody –

ANDY: You told me innit.

IRENE: – for eleven years you couldn't get a peep out of me
and they tried everything love and money sweets presents
day trips beatings the strap the slipper a cornucopia, now
that is a good word a cornucopia of amateur tortures
nowadays they'd have me swimming with dolphins off
Lindisfarne not that I'd jump in the North Sea just like

that oh no I'd have to be pushed I've been to Bridlington
there's sewage rolling up the beach though it's not as bad
as it was – nineteen to twenty-nine I didn't say a word now
you guess why I'll give you a clue – sex.

(*ANDY turns and addresses JUDITH.*)

ANDY: (*To JUDITH.*) I got a flat now. Seventeen B Mavis Road.

JUDITH: Mavis Road. But that's just round the corner. That's
smashing. What have you got?

ANDY: One room over a garage. It was the garage I wanted.
It's a granny flat innit but she died.

(*JUDITH and ANDY look at IRENE.*)

IRENE: Don't look at me – I didn't kill her. Have you got your
own front door? that's what I always ask if you haven't it's
not your own place you're sharing flat A B C D E F G H. I
don't care if you haven't got your own letterbox and your
own front door then you're living in a commune you need
your own roof, front door, and letter box. Have you got a
bell?

ANDY: Yeah.

IRENE: Well I'm glad we sorted that out I was getting a bit
worried for a moment.

JUDITH: That's nice. You being just around the corner.
Stephen will be pleased.

ANDY: Can I get his rasp? He said. I know where it is.

JUDITH: Yes, of course Andrew.

ANDY: Fanks Judith.

(*ANDY exits stage left.*)

IRENE: He's always round here.

JUDITH: He's like a son.

IRENE: No he isn't. If he was like a son he'd have Stephen's
ears, or something. He's not a bit like a son. He's taking
advantage.

JUDITH: He's lost everyone. The least we can do is show
willing.

IRENE: I think he's putting it on.

JUDITH: What do you mean?

IRENE: The moron bit.

JUDITH: He's not a moron.

IRENE: That's what I mean.

    (*Enter ANDY with a rasp in his hand.*)

    You found it then?

ANDY: No.

JUDITH: What are you making Andy?

ANDY: Same fing innit.

IRENE: How are you getting on with your young lady?

ANDY: Alright.

    (*To JUDITH.*) Fought I'd ask you summat. I wanna ask her
    out for a meal.

IRENE: You can't bring her here.

JUDITH: Shh!

IRENE: Don't shush me. What am I a kid?

JUDITH: I'm sorry Irene. I didn't mean it.

    (*IRENE stands.*)

IRENE: Did you get me a book?

JUDITH: They'd sold out.

IRENE: Sold out of Brewer's. They had six copies last week. I
    looked.

JUDITH: Go to the library.

IRENE: (*To ANDY.*) I'm going. Two can play the reservations
    game you know.

    (*IRENE exits stage left.*)

ANDY: I wanna get her a present, and then ask her out mebbe.

JUDITH: Oh, you haven't been out with her yet? I thought –

ANDY: I've talked wiv her.

    (*JUDITH stands and walks to centre stage.*)

JUDITH: I don't think you should buy a present as the first
    thing you do. After you've had a date. That'd be nice, and
    normal.

ANDY: Invite her for dinner then? Cook for her?

JUDITH: No. That'd be too forward. It would mean her having
    to go to your place, your garage.

    (*JUDITH paces, thinking.*)

ANDY: There's a bedroom and kitchen upstairs.

JUDITH: That's what I mean. You can't ask a girl –

ANDY: A woman.

JUDITH: A woman you don't know, into what is your
bedroom, it would look terrible, and you can't cook
anyway.

ANDY: Why would it look terrible?

JUDITH: You have to make a girl feel safe. She has to feel that
she can leave anytime, if she really has to, you know. If
she's on your territory then you're at an advantage, aren't
you?

ANDY: That's why I fought it'd be a good idea.

JUDITH: If you're trying to take advantage of her Andrew I
can't give you any advice.

ANDY: She's older than me. It's not as if she don't know what
she wants.

*(ANDY stands and walks behind JUDITH and takes the post from
his jacket and puts it back on to the coffee table.)*

JUDITH: Oh God. How old is she?

ANDY: Firty-five. I dunno. How do you tell?

JUDITH: Heavens. She is a lot older than you.

ANDY: If I tell her it's a garage wiv a kitchen and bedroom
over it, she'll know the score won't she. So if she don't
wanna come then it's up to her ain't it?

JUDITH: I suppose if you put it like that, yes. Where did you
meet her?

ANDY: I know her. But I still can't cook, yeah.

JUDITH: There's not much you can do about that.

ANDY: You could cook for me, yeah. Come round and do the
cooking. I'd pay you.

JUDITH: Ha! Get a take-away for heaven's sake.

ANDY: Na. I want the kitchen to smell, like I been cooking.
Like I've put a bit of effort in.

JUDITH: I can't get involved Andrew. I don't want to get
involved.

ANDY: You come round do the cooking, then go, and then she
comes round an hour later. I just keep everfing warm in the
oven.

(ANDY comes to centre stage and faces JUDITH.)

JUDITH: I just get out of the way before the sex starts. Ha!
You've got a nerve.

(*Pause.*)

ANDY: I'm sorry Judith. I didn't mean to embarrass you. I fought I could talk to you about fings like this.

JUDITH: You can Andrew, you can.

(*ANDY sits.*)

ANDY: I've never done it you see.

JUDITH: Oh my God. You're a virgin?

ANDY: Yeah. Not the whole way, no, never.

JUDITH: Goodness. Does this woman know you're a virgin?

ANDY: Yeah.

JUDITH: You've told her? Gosh. How did you manage that?

ANDY: Dunno. Just came out.

JUDITH: Who is she?

ANDY: I don't wanna tell you.

JUDITH: Does she live round here?

ANDY: Yeah.

JUDITH: How do you know that she likes you?

ANDY: Obvious innit?

JUDITH: Is it?

ANDY: Yeah. She smiles at me.

JUDITH: Well I smile at everyone. Our mothers always taught us to smile, even if there's nothing to smile about. I still do that. It looks a bit stupid sometimes I know, but I can't stop. If she smiles at you it might not mean what you want it to mean. She's trying to look attractive, nice.

(*Pause.*)

ANDY: I've been finking about fings. Bin getting me down it has. Depression innit. Finking about ways of topping myself.

JUDITH: Oh my God. I'm sorry love. I didn't know. Sex isn't everything Andrew. Love is, love's, love – it's better if there's love.

ANDY: Have you ever done it wiv anyone you didn't, you know, love?

JUDITH: In Poland, yes. (*Beat.*)

I'll cook. But I don't want to meet her.

ANDY: Fanks Judith.

JUDITH: What do you want me to cook?

ANDY: Dunno.

JUDITH: What do you like?

ANDY: Veggie innit.

JUDITH: Is she vegetarian?

ANDY: Na.

JUDITH: You don't want anything too heavy. Ha! Listen to me! Fish or pasta. Are you OK with fish?

ANDY: I fink she likes fish. I'll just eat the veg. Don't worry about it.

JUDITH: How about trout in garlic, oh no, maybe not garlic; cod in a rich; no nothing too rich; ah! salmon in a red pepper, mild pepper, sauce. Perfect. Get a nice bottle of white wine.

ANDY: Yeah. Great. Fanks Judith.

JUDITH: Do you know what always works for me? I shouldn't be telling you this!

ANDY: Go on.

JUDITH: Dessert wine. My favourite is Montbassillac. Tips you over the edge from good behaviour into the land of the extremely irresponsible! Ha! Listen to me. We, me and Steve, first started having Montbassillac wine when we toured Picardy.

ANDY: Where's that?

JUDITH: France. The Somme. Fifteen cemeteries, sixteen if you count Arras, though it's not really Picardy. Yes, you need more than a fortnight. That was where the twins were conceived.

ANDY: Fanks Judith. I'll buy all the gear, and I let you know when. Like I said I'll pay you.

JUDITH: No, no. We'll see.

ANDY: Ta.

(*ANDY walks down-stage and the lights focus on him. He is on his mobile phone. He takes a bank statement from his pocket. He taps in a series of numbers using the keypad whilst listening to instructions from the other end. He taps in a second shorter string of numbers and then he's through.*)

ANDY: (*On the phone.*) Stephen Winston Rudyard Horatio England...eleven, six, nineteen fifty-five...Padgett...

Gizmo...yeah...firty from the cashpoint on the corner of Church Street, Saturday about two.

(*The light spreads to show STEPHEN entering from stage left and taking a position centre stage with his back to the audience. He is naked. During the next, he urinates on the floor centre stage.*)

I wanna make a BACS payment to a company? Yeah, great. Two fousand to Ark Renovations, that's A R K Renovations, HSBC account number 9086 4532 1888, sort code 44 23 45. ...Good. And anofer fing, I wanna change my code word? It come out in the pub innit? ...Lucerne, like the lake OK? Great, fanks. (*He flips the mobile closed.*)

(*To black and end of first half.*)

ACT TWO

The same. IRENE is downstage left. She is talking to the librarian.

IRENE: Young man that copy of Brewer's Dictionary of Phrase
and Fable there it says it's a reference book only now
what exactly does that mean does it mean that I can only
refer to it here and that I can't take it out on loan if that's
the case then this isn't a lending library at all what you're
saying is that I can come round when it suits you and
look something up during hours that suit you when I need
Brewer's round the clock, and I mean need it, I do need
it. I'm not just your average customer who watches Match
of the Day and wants to know what early doors means or
where it came from I think it goes back to the days when
they used to send someone round to knock on the doors
of factory workers that was before alarm clocks I'm only
guessing I haven't looked it up myself I was using that as
an example only I don't use Brewer's like most people use
Brewer's I need a copy and for some reason which I'm
trying to work out there's none in the shops even though
this is a university town mind you it's all engineering and
purple nylon tracksuits, though I've got nothing against
nylon myself though I wouldn't choose it for sheets,
there's a hierarchy in sheets isn't there silk, linen, cotton,
polycotton, and nylon you look like a polycotton man to
me that's not a criticism so am I everyone is nowadays
except those young single people who read magazines
but maybe they don't exist I've never met one. You see,
you've got no problem lending out the Delia Smiths even
though they come back all cacked up with eggy bread but
you won't lend the Brewer's. Now ask yourself – is that any
way to run a lending library? (*Beat.*)
I…need…that…book. I can't tell you why, I don't
know you that well love, but mark my words, I'll be
unrecognisable in a week if I can't take it home with
me now. I'm not above stealing you know. Oh no. And

another thing, you've got Under Milk Wood in poetry
when it's a play, a play for voices, I should know.
(*IRENE turns away and heads up-stage left. STEPHEN is
downstage right, standing and reading aloud from the local
Loughborough newspaper.*)

STEPHEN: I did not write this – filth. If you want someone to
take a leak on the mat – I'm your man, but this, no. Listen.
(*Reading.*) Dear Editor, In my work as a Representative
for English Gypsum I have met many people sporting
– bloody hell – sporting poppies as a so-called mark of
respect for those servicemen and women whose lives have
been wasted in the armed conflicts of this century. Wars
which this country has either started or, by its policy of
eschewing – eschewing? You see, not my sort of word is
it? – (*Reading.*) eschewing compromise has prolonged.
Most of the dead were not heroes, and many were even
mendacious cowards. My own father surrendered to the
Germans in North Africa knowing that he would spend the
rest of the war enjoying the loose discipline of the Italian
Prisoner of War system. I say let's forget, and live in peace.
Yours sincerely, Stephen England, Loughborough, name
and address supplied. They didn't print the address, not in
that one, but they did in this one!
(*STEPHEN produces another paper.*)
We'll get firebombed. Bloody local Advertiser. It's run by
two budgies and an ex-miner. I've met him. He's about as
sharp as a round table.
(*STEPHEN sits and talks to his therapist.*)
Who is doing this to me!? Who knows about my dad
and Italy? Me, Judith, anyone who's ever talked to my
mother. Bloody hell! These are her sort of words. Big ones.
She reads a lot of poetry, she has to, she had a thing as
a kid. Have I told you about that? She got raped by two
squaddies on VE night. Then she stopped talking for ten,
eleven years. Silent as the bloody grave. The doctors gave
her a chocolate any time she even looked like opening
her mouth. The doctor was reading poetry to her, and she
got chocolates when she read poetry, to herself that is, not

out loud. And then, the big day, 25th January 1954. Her
first word in ten years. She said 'Waldo' in a Welsh accent.
'Waldo, Waldo, Waldo.' Which is a word from Under Milk
Wood, by that Welsh drunk. So she gets to talking again
and Dad comes home from Italy in 1955. That must of
been a shock for him. She's built like a bus, an eighteen
stone chocolate bus what talks rubbish. I don't know how
Dad ever managed it, you know, for me to come along. He
was probably trying to shut her up. Might have been rape
again, I dunno. (*Beat.*)
Of course, he got sick of her and fucked off. It's the oldest
love story there is. He ended up logging in Burma.
(*STEPHEN is seated down-stage right reading his post. JUDITH
is sat at the sewing machine but not working. IRENE is sat in
her chair. They are all watching TV, Morse. Morse is talking
to Lewis.*)

IRENE: I like a good Morse. Lewis is not as stupid as you think
you know he just looks stupid and does stupid things.
Maybe he is stupid. That Andrew hasn't been round for
a while I don't entirely trust that boy he's not what he
seems he knows that Under Milk Wood is a play and not
a poem now you wouldn't think that someone like that
would know that much about literature I mean explain that
if you can I can't and I've been thinking about it a great
deal I wonder what he's building with your tools I've got
a bad feeling about that. I wouldn't let him in the house.
The woman in the book shop said a young man with a
silly hat had cleaned them out of Brewer's. Now what
would a young man with a silly hat want with six copies
of Brewer's? You'd think one would be enough for most
purposes. I like this kind of television, something you can
get your teeth into. The solicitor did this one. I've seen it
before.

STEPHEN: Bloody hell!
(*STEPHEN stands. The TV is turned off.*)
JUDITH: I was enjoying that.

STEPHEN: You can't enjoy anything in this house. Go on Mum, you might as well tell me the football score, spoil it for me now.

IRENE: You've told me not to tell you the football though if I were you I wouldn't bother you'll only get upset they're not the same without that Muslim lad

STEPHEN: See? That's the football gone now. Why are you doing this to me mother? You write a disgusting letter to the press, sign it from me, you ruin my Morse, and my football. Morse is the only decent thing on telly.

JUDITH: What's on BBC2?

STEPHEN: Some teenager farting the national anthem I shouldn't wonder. What is going on mother?

IRENE: I never wrote any letter you know I didn't.

STEPHEN: Nobody else knows those sort of words. Eschewing and mendacious. You've got a draw full of words like that, all primed and ready to go off.

IRENE: Why would I want to write to the press?

(*During the next STEPHEN paces and frets.*)

STEPHEN: You're dead against me. You didn't even approve of me getting the gong either. Your own son, going to Buckingham Palace meeting the Queen and getting a citizen's bravery award. Did you come to London? Did you come to the function? Did you want to be photographed with the 'human bridge', the man who sacrificed, nearly sacrificed, his own life to save the lives of five children?

IRENE: You've got a bad back, you've had disc trouble –

STEPHEN: Shutup! You not only do not come to London with me but you make a point of smashing up that picture of me with the Queen, what five or six – see, I've lost bloody count of the number of times I've had to get that thing reframed. Deliberate sabotage – that's your game. When was the last time we had a proper two minute silence on Remembrance Sunday eh? Never! One day this house will manage a proper two minute silence. A one hundred and twenty second silence, and not one interrupted by jabber from you. What was it this year?

IRENE: A party popper.

STEPHEN: I know, I bloody know! A bloody party popper.
Last year, thirty seconds in and what do we get? 'Electricity
consumption surges after this because everyone puts
the kettle on.' (*Shouting.*) A PROPER, RESPECTFUL, TWO
MINUTE CONTEMPLATION FOR THE BLOODY HEROIC
DEAD! Let's do it now. Let's just see if for the first time in
ten years we can pull it off. Jude! Stop that. Two minutes
from now.

(*Silence. At the beginning of the silence STEPHEN is standing
centre stage, JUDITH is sitting at the sewing machine, IRENE
is in her armchair. STEPHEN stands looking at his watch. He
glares at IRENE occasionally. IRENE looks mischievous. And
STEPHEN polices her more intensely. After a minute IRENE
makes a movement with her arm as if to raise a point or
objection. STEPHEN dives in grabs her arm and clamps his
hand over her mouth. He now has his right hand clamped over
her mouth and is checking his watch with the left. The phone
rings. STEPHEN panics. He knows that if he doesn't answer
the phone the answerphone will kick in with his voice. He
gesticulates to JUDITH to answer the phone, but JUDITH doesn't
fully understand what to do – his miming is all panic and no
communication. The answerphone comes on after four rings. The
answerphone starts with the music from the Dam Busters and
then STEPHEN's own voice in a cod version of a squadron leader
begins. Dam Busters music is under.*)

ANSWERPHONE: Squadron Leader Stephen England here,
24 thousand feet over the drink at the mo, damned
inconvenient for all concerned, leave name rank and
number and I'll give you a bell when back in Blighty. Tally
ho, roger, over and out.

(*More and louder Dam Busters music and then a beep.*)

VOICE OF BILL: (*On the phone.*) It's Bill here from the British
Legion. Er, we've seen your letter in the Advertiser, and
er, obviously not happy about it. We've had an EGM and
there was a unanimous vote to issue an EMS on your er,
membership, and suspend your activities vis à vis your tour
secretary role on the Normandy trip, and the darts, that is

captaincy of the darts team. Er...we feel let down matey.
That's the top and bottom of it. Er, that's it. Thank you.

STEPHEN: Bugger!

(*He lets go of IRENE and stands and stares at the answerphone.*)
Bugger!

IRENE: You're talking! He's talking.

STEPHEN: You've got me banned from the bloody British
Legion now!

IRENE: Bravery award? I never believed it. You used to cry if
you fell over.

STEPHEN: Mother, please!

IRENE: I think that Andrew is up to something.

(*STEPHEN covers his ears, and continues reading his post.*)
The boy in the library said that every copy of Brewer's in
Leicestershire was out on loan and also reserved which she
had to admit was very unusual and that book shop with the
coffee in it didn't have any new ones and none in stock –

(*STEPHEN stands suddenly holding a letter.*)
– mind you I don't know what I'd do starting from scratch,
without the underlinings I'm lost, I've got a system you
know –

STEPHEN: What!? The bastards! They've bounced three
cheques. Insufficient funds. I've got a grand in there. What
the f–

(*He rings his bank on the phone. He keys in his bank account
number and sort code.*)
Evening love, now look here you've bounced three
cheques, oh bloody hell, alright, alright... Stephen Winston
Rudyard Horatio England...Padgett... Gizmo... What? No,
I haven't... Well what have I changed it to? ...Why can't
you tell me? ...I have not changed my bloody password...
Oh sod off!

(*He puts the phone down. And sits staring at the ceiling.*)

JUDITH: You should have more respect for the women who
work in those call centres! You don't know how upsetting
abuse like that can be.

(*Enter ANDY from stage left carrying the rasp.*)
Andrew?

ANDY: I brought his rasp back.

STEPHEN: Stop right there pal!

JUDITH: Stephen!

STEPHEN: Someone's been fucking about with my bank account and if it's not any of us it must be him. The little toe rag.

ANDY: I fink I'd better go Jude.

STEPHEN: Jude? Jude? I'm the only person who can call that woman Jude.

ANDY: She said innit.

STEPHEN: I don't care what she bloody said, I'm telling you. Now sit your arse down and shutup.

IRENE: Have you been going around the book shops –

STEPHEN: Shut the fuck up mother!

(*Silence. STEPHEN stands and paces.*)

Right. Now then, horror bollocks, like I say, someone's been fucking about with my money. Someone who has access to my post, which we stupidly leave kicking around. According to this I have made a payment of two thousand pounds to 'Ark Renovations' of Goole – whoever they are, and consequently my account is up the Swanny. Well?

ANDY: That'll be for the yacht then innit?

(*Pause.*)

STEPHEN: You what?

ANDY: Ark Renovations is that boat yard at Goole where we had a look at the different boats innit. You put a deposit down on that fibre glass yacht. Two hundred and twennie quid. The two fousand'll be the difference?

IRENE: A yacht! Oh that's nice, we can all go sailing now.

JUDITH: What have you done Steve?

(*STEPHEN sits.*)

STEPHEN: I dunno.

ANDY: We went up to Goole last month when his rugby was cancelled and looked around this boatyard. They're second and fird hand yachts, but this Ark Renovations does 'em up innit. He took a fancy to this fibre glass one.

JUDITH: You didn't tell me you went to Goole.

STEPHEN: I've never been to bloody Goole! What is Goole?

IRENE: I hope it floats. What colour is it Stephen?

STEPHEN: What colour is it? I don't know.

(*IRENE stands and goes to the coffee table. She picks up the pile of old post, the junk mail section, and sits down with it again.*)

IRENE: I'm sure I saw a picture of a yacht in the post. I didn't think anything of it at the time. When you live in Loughborough you don't think about the sea much. Full fathom five my father lies…that's alliteration, quite a lot of alliteration actually, too much for my liking – and there's a half rhyme with five and lies, and my come to think of it. It's endless – poetry – if you keep looking and count all the halves.

JUDITH: (*Snapping.*) Irene!

(*JUDITH sits on the arm of STEPHEN's chair and puts an arm around him. STEPHEN is just staring at the floor. IRENE picks out a letter from the wad.*)

IRENE: Here we go. Ark Renovations, Wharf Road, Goole. Received from Stephen England, two hundred and twenty pounds as deposit for the purchase of 'Cassandra' – daughter of Priam and Hecuba, she was, no one believed a thing she said – ha! I know how she feels. To be delivered, on January the twenty-eighth, to 1 Corona Drive, Loughborough, on receipt of a bank transfer of the balance two thousand pounds.

JUDITH: What's the date on it Irene?

IRENE: January eighteenth. My birthday.

JUDITH: Yes, the pitch was too hard because of the ice. But you said you just stayed at the club drinking, all day.

STEPHEN: I did. I bloody did.

IRENE: So how come you were in Goole buying a yacht then?

JUDITH: You went with him Andrew? You didn't tell me.

ANDY: He said to keep it a secret like. He said you wouldn't fink it was a good idea.

JUDITH: Why did he take you with him?

ANDY: For a laugh innit. I wanted a go in the Alfa. We did hundred and firty on the A1M in fird gear.

STEPHEN: You can't do a hundred and firty, thirty – God! in fird!

ANDY: We did. Try it. Betcha. Look, I'd better be off. I just
  brought the rasp back.
  (*STEPHEN stands.*)
STEPHEN: What else do you want to borrow you bloody
  commie? Workmate, sander, electronic screwdriver, socket
  set, araldite, tile cutter, tile jig, Stanley knife, fish hooks,
  dibble stick –
JUDITH: Shutup Steve.
ANDY: I need an electric glue gun, bandsaw, and a G clamp.
  (*Pause.*)
JUDITH: You've got G clamps haven't you Steve?
STEPHEN: Yeah, loads. What size?
ANDY: Big un.
STEPHEN: Right.
  (*STEPHEN sets off heading for the garage which is off stage left,
  before he exits he turns and addresses ANDY.*)
  I don't have a band saw, or an electronic glue gun. Never
  have had. In fact I don't know anybody who's got a band
  saw and or an electronic glue gun. You're moving from
  DIY into uncharted waters there sunshine. Big G clamp?
  (*STEPHEN exits to the garage via the kitchen.*)
ANDY: Jude, can you do tomorrow night wiv the salmon,
  please?
JUDITH: Oh gosh. What's that? Saturday night. With your
  friend? I don't know Andrew.
ANDY: You said innit? I've told her. She's up for it.
JUDITH: Up for it? Oh my God.
ANDY: Here's twenny for the food and there'll be another
  twenny for your time, yeah?
JUDITH: I don't want paying. It doesn't seem right.
ANDY: Well I want you to get somefin out of it.
  (*Pause.*)
JUDITH: I don't need paying. Are you nervous?
ANDY: Me? Yeah.
JUDITH: Don't be nervous. It'll be alright. It'll only be not
  alright if you're nervous.
ANDY: I'll have a drink innit.
JUDITH: Yes, but not too much. Just enough. Gosh.

(*Enter STEPHEN carrying a large G clamp. He slaps it into ANDY's outstretched hand.*)

STEPHEN: This is gonna be one helluva bloody cheese board this is.

ANDY: It's nearly finished. I'll invite you round.

IRENE: It's Friday today. Are you still wearing what you like on Fridays Andrew?

ANDY: No.

IRENE: I don't know what that means with him.

ANDY: I'm off. (*To JUDITH.*) Tomorrow? Yeah?

JUDITH: Yes.

(*ANDY exits stage left.*)

STEPHEN: (*To IRENE.*) Tomorrow? What's that about?

(*STEPHEN doesn't listen to IRENE.*)

IRENE: He wants Judith to go round and cook a dinner for him and his older lady friend he's trying to seduce her, Judith that is if you ask me, but that's only my intuition and although I'm usually right I can't be sure but I am absolutely positive that it's Andrew who's going around buying Brewer's Phrase and Fables. There isn't a single copy in the Midlands you know not even paperback, they're going to send one down from Bangor which is Wales of course. My uncle Clarrie told me never to trust a Welshman, and he should know – he was from Swansea.

STEPHEN: Jude! What the bloody hell is happening tomorrow?!

JUDITH: (*Angry.*) We are taking delivery of a yacht.

(*Lights focus on STEPHEN in the therapist's chair.*)

STEPHEN: It was like a bloody stable in Bethlehem. They're all queueing up to have a go. Every Tom, Dick and bloody Harry shoving their hairy arms up my wife, having a good rummage around, and then declaring that they'd like so-and-so's opinion. And when it did start happening – fuck – I was down the wrong end pal. I tell you if you ever – ah, well maybe not. The thing is I'd fainted at the amnio whachamicallit. I'd gone in to hold her hand, you know, and then this bloke gets this flagpole of a needle out of a bag and I've keeled over on the tiles, blood everywhere.

They had to call the cleaners. So what made me think I
could hack the birth I do not know. She had to be cut and
stitched an' all. Ugh. I felt like an extra on the set of the
Exorcist. I would have preferred a caesarian – at least the
put a curtain across and there's an excuse for not looking.
Anyhow, home. First six months, didn't think about it, you
know, twins, too busy. Next six months same, nothing.
But Jude did. I could tell, but she didn't talk about it. I'd
stopped touching her, didn't cuddle her, no squeezes. I just
couldn't imagine it. I've always thought – how do those
monks hold out? I used to think they cheated, you know,
crafty, knock one out in the orchard or summat, but now I
understand, it's not that difficult really, if you can't imagine
doing it, you don't miss it. So, how old are the twins? Six.
Six years. Bloody hell. I feel like a virgin.

(*Lights spread, but still low. ANDY and JUDITH are centre stage.
The chairs are not lit.*)

JUDITH: It's quite nice Andrew. I was expecting a garage.

ANDY: Garage is downstairs innit.

JUDITH: But the garage is in the rent?

ANDY: Yeah. I got mi wood in there ain't I.

JUDITH: Of course. How is that going? The wood.

ANDY: Alright.

JUDITH: Must be a lot easier. Having the space I mean. For
woodworking.

ANDY: Yeah, I can walk about now innit.

JUDITH: What are you making Andy?

ANDY: Nofin much.

JUDITH: I bet it's a table. Do you have any heating?

ANDY: No. I don't mind the cold. Not when I'm working.

JUDITH: I mean up here.

ANDY: Yeah. There's heating.

JUDITH: Is it on?

ANDY: No. I'll put it on yeah?

JUDITH: (*Giggling.*) Well it's not for me to say but I wouldn't
even take my coat off in here, never mind, you know.

ANDY: You're a good cook yeah?

JUDITH: I'm a bit worried about that oven Andrew. Have you used it at all yet?

ANDY: Na.

JUDITH: And it needs a clean. She'll think you don't care. Dirty.

ANDY: You're a bit old fashioned for a woman aren't you? Like them photographs you see of women in dresses, in kitchens.

JUDITH: I'm not going to let myself be bullied into doing things which don't make me happy if that's what you mean. I work twenty hours a week at the call centre, so I never have to ask Steve for any money for myself. I look after twin girls and that's very hard, and skilled work. I am not running the United Nations, no. I've done that. Not the United Nations, obviously – United Sugars. You're not listening are you?

ANDY: Sorry.

JUDITH: Listening is the most important thing you can do with a woman.

ANDY: Yeah?

JUDITH: Better than having a car, or being funny. Listening. I was anybody's in my twenties as long as they nodded every now and then.

ANDY: I'm sorry.

JUDITH: You're miles away aren't you?

ANDY: I been working. Had a good day. Got a lot done.

JUDITH: The wood.

ANDY: Yeah.

JUDITH: It's nice that you've got an interest.

ANDY: Sorry.

JUDITH: I was going to tell you about when I worked for United Sugars in Poland, but you're obviously still downstairs mentally – bevelling.

ANDY: I don't bevel anyfing. Don't seem right.

JUDITH: You accused me of being – stupid. I have a degree in Polish.

ANDY: That's a difficult language innit?

JUDITH: Not if you're Polish. I'm a quarter Polish, Jewish
Polish – it's very complicated. I lived in Krakow after
University and became fluent, well you know that.

ANDY: Hippies.

JUDITH: It's a shame there's not that sort of thing for young
people nowadays. For people like you. Mind you, you've
got your wood.

ANDY: I need to get a window in downstairs.

JUDITH: You've got electricity haven't you?

ANDY: Course. But I want a big window. Light.

JUDITH: You'll need planning permission for that. People don't
like to think that they're being watched.

ANDY: It's big enough down there, but I need better light.

JUDITH: Can you do the sawing in the garden?

ANDY: (*Snort of derision.*) Joke.

JUDITH: You want it all to be private don't you?

ANDY: So?

JUDITH: It's not a table then. I don't like being watched doing
anything. Puts me off. That's not true, I can sew, material
I'm confident with material, anything else and I get put
off. I seize up – mentally. You got a lot of space sometimes
squatting. I learnt a lot about plumbing, and electricity. I've
forgotten it all now of course. I made the curtains. Made
all the curtains. A lot of people say all kinds of things about
squatting but for me it was like running a bloody curtain
factory.

ANDY: You swore.

JUDITH: Did I? What did I say?

ANDY: Bloody curtain factory.

JUDITH: Huh, I was a bloody curtain factory. I was exploited. I
must be upset.

ANDY: What happened with the sugar factory?

JUDITH: Plant. Not factory. Sugar beet is a root crop. You
make sugar from it, you can't manufacture sugar. United
Sugars sent me back to Poland, to the northern Gladvik
plains to set up a sugar beet processing plant. On my own.
I was twenty-seven. Not much older than you. It was an

investment of seventeen million pounds. Me and three
hundred Polish men.

ANDY: Is that like desert, them plains?

JUDITH: No, but it is flat. All Poland is flat. That's why they've
been invaded so often. It's like one big field.

ANDY: I like the sound of deserts. Where's the nearest desert
Jude?

JUDITH: Derby. Ha!

ANDY: I like Derbyshire. The Peak district, caves, stuff. It's shit
round here, there's noffin.

JUDITH: Well there's nothing in a desert.

ANDY: Yeah, but what you want is either noffin or somefin.
When there's noffin at all – there's somefin – there's like
…noffin big time. It's being in the middle, like here, which
is shit, cos there's noffin.

JUDITH: I should be cooking. It's all done anyway.

ANDY: Go on. I wanna know what happens.

JUDITH: I had an office in an old sewage works.

ANDY: Yeah?

JUDITH: Yes. You see that's were the squatting came in. I could
improvise. It didn't bother me. Just one big lovely office
with lots of plants, and armchairs. And the sun came in
late afternoon, yes, you'd like that, lots of light, too much
actually.

ANDY: How tall was the room?

JUDITH: The ceilings? Tall – about fifteen foot. Yes, they were
very high ceilings, and huge windows of course. Eight foot
six drop on the windows.

ANDY: Fuck!

JUDITH: Yes. It was quite a place. Everything went fantastically
well. Then we started recruiting staff and the Polish
management did the interviews and offered the jobs.
They'd set up a six day shift system, Sunday to Friday,
but got everyone to sign a contract to say that if they had
to they would be willing to work a shift on the Saturday.
I looked at the names on the rejected application forms.
Brunfeld, Gerthauser, Schwarz. The Jews couldn't sign the
Saturday clause, so they didn't get offered jobs. I knew all

about it. I wasn't involved, unless I wanted to get involved. I even thought of it as a skill. You know, being aware of local customs, traditions, and respecting them. Ha! I think I know what I should have done, but I wasn't interested. I left after eighteen months. I got a taxi to the airport. The driver was Harold Lieberman. He'd applied for a job at the plant. He had three jobs, worked sixteen hours a day, and earned about half what he would earn at the plant for an ordinary week. I suppose I wish it hadn't happened like that but it did.

ANDY: Is the sewage works still there?

JUDITH: No, we knocked it down. We needed the hard core.

ANDY: (*He kisses his teeth – cod Jamaican.*)

JUDITH: Those sorts of things can get very complex once you get involved. But there's not many people who have set up a sugar beet processing plant in Poland Andrew, men or women, and no one can take that away from me.

ANDY: You fucked up though didn't yer?

JUDITH: (*Fighting back tears.*) I wished I'd done it properly, but I couldn't, I didn't want to upset anyone, so I upset myself instead. I'm sorry I'd better go.

ANDY: No. Don't go Jude. Please innit.

JUDITH: I look at photographs of me then and I think I'm looking at another woman. I wish she'd been stronger, bigger, better than she was, and I wished she'd done the job properly, but she didn't, and I don't think anybody could have. Ha! Anyway, that's gone.

(*ANDY walks to centre stage and stands close to her.*)

ANDY: Forget it.

JUDITH: I wish I hadn't told you.

ANDY: I mean, I don't fink I like you any less cos of what you done.

JUDITH: That's kind of you Andrew. Thank you for listening. If I were you I'd ask Stephen about a window for the garage. He's very good at planning permission. He can get you discounts on a frame too. He knows everyone. Now then, what time is your friend supposed to be arriving?

ANDY: You're my friend Jude.

JUDITH: Yes, I suppose you could say I was a friend. A
friend who had just come round to see you, to do a bit of
cleaning.
(*ANDY takes a hold of JUDITH's waist.*)
Andrew?! What is it?

ANDY: I fink we should kiss.
(*Pause.*)

JUDITH: You mean I'm your friend friend? Oh goodness me.
Gosh. It had crossed my mind but I thought – Oh sugar!
Sorry, I didn't mean to swear.

ANDY: Sugar!

JUDITH: Yes, sugar! It's all sugar tonight isn't it?! Oh shit!
(*Lights spread to take in STEPHEN in the therapist's rooms. He
is kneeling on the floor. He has been crying.*)

STEPHEN: Oh God. Oh fucking hell. I'm sorry. Oh, bloody
hell. And I said you'd never hypnotise me! Not in a million
years. Did you have me snogging a fire extinguisher like
they do on telly? Oh my good God. Do I get to keep the
tape or do you play it for a laugh at psychiatric dinner
parties?
(*During the next, ANDY kisses JUDITH gently on the lips. It is
a relatively short kiss and she stands stiffly with her eyes closed.
She then relaxes and her body flops into his and she kisses him
passionately on the lips. He pulls her cardigan off of her, and
she lifts his sweatshirt over his head and kisses his chest. These
actions are done sensuously and slowly, and not in a frenzied
manner. They discard JUDITH's cardigan on the floor and they
exit stage right.*)
I'd blacked out then. That's why I couldn't remember. The
memory got trapped in the nervous system. Didn't get
filed. Paperwork. Never been my thing. I'll have to give
my gong back. Just stick it in a jiffy bag and send it back to
Westminster. My mum never believed it. She always said
with my back, my dodgy discs, I could never have done it.
Do you think I should tell the police? What we don't know
though is whether Andy knows anything. He must know
that his dad was the bridge man, not me. Oh bloody hell.
I'm disgusted. I am so disgusted. Maybe he blacked out

too. Do you think I should ask him? We've never really talked about it. I mean, what if he knows?

(*IRENE is down-stage left talking to a shop assistant.*)

IRENE: (*With growing desperation.*) Brewer's Dictionary of Phrase and Fable. You had fifteen on the computer in December. I always ask. I get it wrong sometimes and call it Phrase and Phrabel. It's like Cane and Abel, two sons, one of them killed the other. Cane's the killer. I remember that by imagining Cane killing Abel with a specially sabotaged cane chair. That's not how he did it but it helps me to remember who was the killer which is useful although unfortunately I never trust wicker furniture myself anymore that would be a terrible way to go wouldn't it? That's called a mnemonic. Elephants Are Ugly that's a mnemonic. I use that to remember how to spell beautiful. EAU Elephants are ugly. I've forgotten how you spell mnemonic. If Abel had been called rock like Rock Hudson the mnemonic wouldn't work. You could kill someone with a rock you see. But Rock didn't do it Cane did. There's something wrong there oh fiddle when it happens it's a big drop like falling off a waterfall it's not gradual they all just go one minute they're there and the next I'm back to nothing that's why the underlining's important the key words are like the buttons on a sofa you know where you are if there were no buttons on a sofa it'd be like those salt flats where they do the land speed record you'd get lost wandering about not knowing where you are and then without any warning at all you'd be knocked down by someone doing three hundred miles an hour they say if they hit a fly at that speed it's like hitting the side of a house I've never believed that sort of rubbish they make it up to make their lives more exciting I'll wait yes I'll wait. (*Silence.*)

You don't have any. That's me then. There were fifteen in December. A young man bought all fifteen at once? What was he wearing? Really. It must have been a Friday then. (*Lights spread to take in JUDITH, alone at her table. She is still, frozen. Enter STEPHEN from stage left. He is energised.*)

56

STEPHEN: Jude?

JUDITH: (*Not looking at him.*) Yes?

STEPHEN: Jude?

JUDITH: What?

STEPHEN: There are suitcases in the hall.

JUDITH: Yes. And there's a yacht in the drive.

STEPHEN: Is there? I didn't see a yacht.

(*STEPHEN goes to stage right and looks.*)

Bloody hell. You get a lodda second hand yacht for two thousand quid don't you. Fuck, I thought it'd be a little one! I didn't even notice it. Has anyone said anything?

(*JUDITH hands him a fax.*)

What's this?

(*He reads it.*)

No, no, no! Oh bloody hell. What a nerve. You don't believe this do you? You can't let yourself believe this. Ha! You godda give it to him – he's creative. Don't even think about it Jude! Last week they didn't even have enough snow to ski never mind get swept away in a bloody avalanche. I'm telling you Jude the twins are fine, they're not dead. No way, forget it.

JUDITH: There's a yacht in the drive isn't there?

STEPHEN: The yacht's easy peasy. I mean – come on Jude. Don't let yourself think this. This is all Andy. You know that don't you?

JUDITH: No.

STEPHEN: I've just got to go and see Andy. You don't understand. It's all Andy. Jude? Look, look, I bet the fax is from that newsagents on the corner, look, the sender's number is always on the top.

(*STEPHEN checks the fax.*)

Yeah, well, he's clever, like I say. He's probably got someone in Austria to send it for him. When did this come? This is stupid Jude. Jude! Look, if the twins were really dead the headmaster wouldn't send a bloody fax would he. Ha! And he wouldn't have any School headed paper with him either. Eh? Course not. It's a joke. Give me a break. It's me he's after. Now Jude, the suitcases – what's all that about?

JUDITH: I slept with him.

STEPHEN: You slept with him?

JUDITH: Yes.

STEPHEN: Where?

JUDITH: In his garage.

STEPHEN: You slept with Andy in that garage in Mavis Road?

JUDITH: Yes.

STEPHEN: He's got a bed in there?

JUDITH: Yes.

STEPHEN: I mean – when you say you slept with him you mean you slept slept with him, as in doing it?

JUDITH: Yes.

STEPHEN: You see, that's it. It's all part of his plan.

JUDITH: You don't care do you?

STEPHEN: Of course I care, but –

JUDITH: You don't fucking care!

STEPHEN: Of course I bloody care, but I know what he's up to. He's just getting at me. He didn't really want to sleep with you.

JUDITH: He wanted to sleep with me, and you don't!

STEPHEN: Oh now come on Jude that's different. That's out of order.

JUDITH: He wanted to sleep with me. He seduced me.

STEPHEN: I know, I know! You're not listening. I bloody know this! I'm telling you why he slept with you.

JUDITH: He wanted me! He wanted me! He wanted me!

(*JUDITH begins to punch STEPHEN about the face. STEPHEN just takes it. He doesn't try to defend himself.*)

STEPHEN: No he doesn't. Stop that Jude! Come on Jude! He did it to get at me.

JUDITH: He wants me! He wants me! He wants me!

STEPHEN: Please Jude. Hang on! Listen! Bloody hell. I'm going round to see him. Don't leave me Jude. It's what happened in Switzerland. Don't go love. You're all I've got you know that. You and the twins.

(*STEPHEN grabs her hands and holds them down. From upstage centre ANDY begins walking downstage pushing a very large, and beautiful sculpture. The sculpture is made from marine ply and*

*is about six foot tall, and looks like an abstract representation
of a vagina or an upright canoe.)*

JUDITH: The twins are dead!

STEPHEN: No they're not. You're not bloody listening are
you?! He's faked the fucking fax. He's a clever little
bastard. I'm going to talk to him. It will be alright. I
promise Jude. It'll be alright.

*(ANDY and the sculpture arrive centre stage. ANDY exits stage
left. JUDITH sits. The scene changes to ANDY's garage.)*

STEPHEN: Andy! Andy!

(Enter ANDY from stage right.)

ANDY: This is the twennie-first century. You email first, you
don't just come round.

STEPHEN: Yeah, ha! – 'course. Bloody hell. What's this when
it's at home? What is it?

ANDY: Sculpture innit.

STEPHEN: Whose is it? Them in the house? You wanna get
them to shift it. They can't decide to rent out their garage
and then still use it themselves can they. What are they?
Osteopaths? They're the worst. No one can have their
cake and bloody eat it. You godda stick up for yourself
in this world sunshine. If they think you've got a taste for
shit they'll keep feeding it you. What is it anyhow? I know
what it looks like. Bloody pervert.

ANDY: I did it.

STEPHEN: What? This isn't the cheese board? Bloody hell. I
thought you was building something. Something, I dunno,
something you could use, something you needed. Bloody
hell. You been wasting your time doing this.

ANDY: Don't you like it?

STEPHEN: Eh?

ANDY: D'you like it?

STEPHEN: I don't know what it is.

ANDY: What's it look like?

STEPHEN: It looks like a canoe. A disgusting canoe.

ANDY: What's disgusting about it?

STEPHEN: Is it supposed to, you know, look like a woman's
fadge?

ANDY: Mebbe.

STEPHEN: Well you made it pal, you should know. I didn't know you was doing this. You done it well actually. How do you get the wood to bend?

ANDY: It's all cut and glued. Thousands of strips innit.

STEPHEN: Where d'yer learn all this?

ANDY: Night class. Nottingham.

STEPHEN: Nottingham! Bloody hell you have been taking risks. You've done a good job. What's the wood?

ANDY: Marine ply.

STEPHEN: Marine ply? What they make boats out of?

ANDY: Yeah.

STEPHEN: Look Andy son, I've had a lot on my mind recently and, well you know, I know you know, I've been going to see someone, a doctor, and he hypnotised me the other day and got me to talk about that day, you know, on the lake.

ANDY: Tea?

STEPHEN: Eh?

ANDY: Cup of tea?

STEPHEN: NO! I don't want any fucking tea! I've come round here to tell you I'm sorry. I know what happened now. I'd blacked out. I've never known. I promise Andy, I've never known. Never. I blacked out. I've had a bloody great lid on it for years.

ANDY: Judith didn't say no to tea.

STEPHEN: I know about that Andy. I know. She told me.

ANDY: You've been neglecting her innit. No jiggy jig for six years. That's a long time wiv no jiggy jig for a good looking woman.

STEPHEN: Look mate, I know about that. It hasn't worked. You fucked her, I know you fucked her, but you've done it to get at me, I know. I wanna tell you what happened that day on the boat. Forget all that other stuff.

ANDY: Bang! Engine room goes up.

STEPHEN: Yeah. I wet myself. Fill my pants. Natural reaction, apparently.

ANDY: The lake's coming in.

STEPHEN: Yeah. We're going down.

ANDY: The front of the boat is in the air.

STEPHEN: We're all thrown against the back wall.

ANDY: I'm clinging on to a fixed table.

STEPHEN: Your dad opens a porthole.

ANDY: He's got his legs hooked onto the bar and his hands on the porthole.

STEPHEN: Three kids crawl along him like a bridge and out.

ANDY: We're going down. The lake's coming in.

STEPHEN: I work my way over to the porthole.

ANDY: I'm watching but I can't move.

STEPHEN: Your sister is on your dad's back.

ANDY: I'm watching.

STEPHEN: I kick her off.

ANDY: She slips under the water.

STEPHEN: I kick your dad's feet away from the bar and work my way up to the porthole.

ANDY: I'm watching.

STEPHEN: I can't get out.

ANDY: His arms are through the hole and you can't get out.

STEPHEN: I bite and chew on his hands, and kick at his back.

ANDY: He slips under.

STEPHEN: I'm through, and out.

ANDY: I'm watching.

STEPHEN: I'm underwater. I don't know whether I'm kicking for the surface or going down.

ANDY: In the bar there's a football. I grab it. I work my way to the porthole, now under water. I crawl out, and holding on to the football I float out.

STEPHEN: I see you. I make a grab for the ball.

ANDY: You grab the ball.

STEPHEN: You hang on. I kick at you.

ANDY: I hang on.

STEPHEN: We break the surface.

ANDY: We're picked up.

STEPHEN: The French kids point me out.

ANDY: It was the jacket.

STEPHEN: A brown leather jacket – like your dad's.

ANDY: English.

STEPHEN: An Englishman in a brown leather jacket.

ANDY: Le monsieur qui a fait le pont.

STEPHEN: (*Crying.*) I blacked out Andy. I didn't know! People told me. I went along with it. For seven years I haven't known. I haven't had a bloody clue! Not til recently. I'm gonna make it up to you kid. I don't care what, I'll make it up to you. What do you want? Andy? I'm asking you sunshine, what do you want?

(*ANDY stares out front. The lights go to black. The lights come up on the three chairs. The sculpture has gone. ANDY's Ikea chair is where STEPHEN's used to be. JUDITH's and IRENE's as before. Silence.*)

IRENE: (*In a welsh accent.*) Waldo!

(*Silence.*)

Waldo!

JUDITH: Do you have to do it in Welsh Irene? It sounds a bit mad when you do it in Welsh, because you're not Welsh. Andrew? Do you think we can give Irene her Brewer's back. Some poetry. At least her Under Milk Wood. This Waldo business is driving me up the wall.

ANDY: Rock and a hard place innit. Waldo or bollocks. Lots of bollocks.

JUDITH: Yes, I suppose I'd forgotten that. I'll give Waldo another month.

IRENE: Waldo!

ANDY: Just ignore it.

JUDITH: I was thinking about a holiday for us. Maybe Tunisia. A beach holiday. It's a Muslim country but very French. The man at the travel agents said you can go topless on the beach all year round except during Ramadhan, which is obviously a lie born of pig ignorance. People will say anything to make a sale nowadays.

ANDY: Yeah, OK. Tunisia. No twins.

JUDITH: What?

ANDY: No twins. Toughen up Jude. He can have them for a fortnight.

JUDITH: We'll have to take Irene. Do you think they'd let her in the country?

ANDY: Why wouldn't they?

IRENE: Waldo!

ANDY: You can't stop people coming into your country just because they've got, like, bad memories. But she ain't coming all the same.

JUDITH: No?

ANDY: No. (*Beat.*) Yeah, let's go to Tunisia.

JUDITH: Oh wonderful Andrew!

(*Enter STEPHEN from stage right.*)

STEPHEN: Hello Jude. Andy. Mum.

IRENE: Waldo!

ANDY: You again eh?

STEPHEN: Yeah. Sorry.

ANDY: On the cadge?

STEPHEN: Yeah.

JUDITH: Would you like a cup of tea Steve?

ANDY: No he don't. He's not stopping.

STEPHEN: Mitre box. I know where it is. I'll get it.

ANDY: Oh no you don't.

JUDITH: How are you getting on Stephen?

STEPHEN: I've finished. Doing the details now. You can improve a garage with the quality of your detailing. Brass door furnishings, decent architrave, windows.

ANDY: They gonna let you put windows in?

STEPHEN: Yeah, one, a little one.

ANDY: What overlooking them?

STEPHEN: Na! Next door's garage.

ANDY: Mitre box?

STEPHEN: Yeah.

(*ANDY exits to the garage.*)

IRENE: Waldo!

STEPHEN: What's happening here?

JUDITH: He took all her books away yesterday. Stripped her room.

STEPHEN: What?! He can't do that!

JUDITH: No chocolates. No books. Except for Waldo, she's stopped talking altogether.

STEPHEN: Yeah? Bloody hell. (*Beat.*)

Why didn't we think of that?

JUDITH: You'll be needing some nets Steve.

STEPHEN: Eh?

JUDITH: Curtains for the window.

STEPHEN: Yeah, I will. Would you?

JUDITH: I'll ask.

STEPHEN: Looks quite nice Jude. I've got rid of the oil off the floor. I'm gonna put terracotta tiles down I think. B and Q. Ambient.

JUDITH: Hard though.

STEPHEN: Oh yes very hard.

(*Enter ANDY carrying a mitre box.*)

ANDY: You got a decent tenon saw?

STEPHEN: I was just gonna use a saw saw.

ANDY: If it's worth doing, it's worth doing well innit.

(*Exit ANDY to garage.*)

STEPHEN: I got sacked. Gypsum sacked me. Using their name in the letter to the papers. Summarily dismissed after nearly twenty years. Remember, the one about not wearing poppies. I didn't even write it. They didn't believe me. Des Stafford sacked me himself. Said he'd stuck his neck out for me time after time, but this was the last straw. He said he thought I was a decent bloke but just a bit shot through, mentally – that was his expression – shot through, mentally. He's alright is Des. He's done the job.

JUDITH: We're going to Tunisia for a beach holiday.

STEPHEN: Oh good. Don't go during Ramadhan.

JUDITH: When is that?

STEPHEN: The ninth month of the Muslim year, but you never know when their year starts. They chop it about. Could be anywhere. They won't tell you either. It's rude to ask. You've got to take pot luck. If you get off the plane, look about and they're all indoors – it's Ramadhan, and you're fucked, basically.

(*Enter ANDY with a tenon saw.*)

ANDY: Here you go.

STEPHEN: Ta.

ANDY: Anyfink else. Jubilee clips, rawl plugs, set square, ladders, ratchet screwdriver, ordinary screwdriver, awl, trench spade –

STEPHEN: What's an awl?

ANDY: The fing what starts you off. Makes a hole for the screw before you screw it.

STEPHEN: Is that what that's called?

ANDY: Yeah.

STEPHEN: Yeah, I could do with one of them.

(*Exit ANDY to garage.*)

It's a bit cold in there Jude. So you're alright here then? He's treating you well is he? Not knocking you about?

JUDITH: He's very gentle.

STEPHEN: Bloody clever git. Knows what he wants don't he? Couldn't have handed the house over with one signature like that if I'd still had a mortgage on this place. Bit of bad luck that.

JUDITH: He is very clever.

(*Enter ANDY with an awl.*)

ANDY: How's it going?

STEPHEN: I'll get myself sorted. Couple of months.

IRENE: Waldo!

STEPHEN: They're not osteopaths you know, in the house.

ANDY: I never thought they were.

STEPHEN: No. That was all me wasn't it. They're acupuncturists which is much the same thing only slightly worse, obviously, cos they're armed.

ANDY: Good luck mate.

STEPHEN: Yeah, ta. Thanks, for the awl.

(*He looks around and then walks off.*)

JUDITH: I'm a bit worried about him.

ANDY: I fink he'll be alright.

IRENE: Waldo!

JUDITH: Can he come to Tunisia? He's never had a holiday. A proper holiday.

ANDY: No. He can look after the twins, and her. Here. For two weeks then he's out again.

(*Pause.*)

At Easter, I'm gonna go to Switzerland. Lake Lucerne. I'll go on my own. There's no need for you or the twins to come. I'll just go like, once, and never again, I promise.

IRENE: Waldo!

(Pause.)
Waldo!
(Pause.)
Waldo!
(To black.)

End.